So, what do you know about being Jewish?

165 Jewish Questions and Answers

Roni Rosenthal

So, What do you know about being Jewish?
copyright © 2010 Roni Rosenthal

Published by StoryTime World Publishing House
info@101letshavefun.com
www.101letshavefun.com

Library of Congress Number : 2010914914
ISBN : 978-09792800-2-3

StoryTime World - publishing house

For my dad:

We miss you.

Contents

Part 2: Jewish Holidays and Symbols

Part 3: Torah and Life Cycle

Part 4: Special Prayers and Blessings

Shalom!

"Who wrote the Torah? What is haftarah? What is inside the mezuzah? Why do we celebrate Lag B'Omer , and who was Theodor Herzl?"

For a Jewish Studies teacher like me, these are very familiar questions. Because there is such a wealth of history and tradition associated with Judaism, it can be hard to know where to start the discussion. Being Jewish defines a relationship to G-d, to your fellow men and women, to Israel, to history, and, just as important, to learning. After all, one of the first things that become obvious when reading the Hebrew Bible is that its heroes and prophets are not supermen. They make mistakes; they have a hard time understanding what G-d wants from them. And that is why the Torah, G-d's law for the Jews, is supported by centuries of scholarship and tradition. Whenever you're struggling to understand something about Judaism, the help is already there, if you know where to look for it. The real trick is where to get started. What's the first question to ask? So, What do *you* know about being Jewish – and how can you start to expand that knowledge?

Over the past five years, I have collected all the questions, debates, and matters for clarification that I have heard from my students and written them down in my journal. I then consulted rabbis (Orthodox, Conservative, and Reform), researched Jewish history books, and consulted with my colleagues, making sure that all my answers were both accurate and complete. It would fill a library to write down everything there is to know about Judaism, but I hope that the questions and answers in this book will enrich your world in the same way that this knowledge enriches mine.

In this book, I present 165 questions and answers. All of these questions have many advantages, including evaluating your knowledge and learning important material in a more fun and memorable way. Also, these questions can serve as a starting point for further research and investigation: after you have learned more about Jewish Arbor Day, for example, you may be interested in checking out the Jewish National Fund's drive to reforest Israel.

It is often said that Jewish people love to answer a question with another question. This is a wise idea! Every new piece of information you uncover can spur you to learn even more. Whether your deepest interest in Judaism is religious, historical, cultural, literary, musical, or all of the above, you will find that Judaism weaves these different strands together with a deftness that can be surprising. For example, a few passages in the Torah about blowing the horns to summon the tribes to worship has been expanded into the vast repertoire of musical modes and styles that professional cantors study to this day. Battles fought hundreds or thousands of years ago that might otherwise be relegated to the footnotes of history books have given life to vibrant traditions and celebrations still observed by Jewish people today, and great historical events from just the past few generations have given rise to new observances and traditions. Every name, every event, and every tiny custom that has become a part of Judaism has great meaning attached to it, and the answers are here – if you are not afraid to ask.

For Jewish teachers and educators, I have attached an appendix to this book with some suggestions for fun learning games using the educational material in this book. I hope, you will be able to use these questions as a starting point to get your students excited about the treasure trove that is Jewish history!

Acknowledgments

I would like to thank my mom, my sister and my adorable kids, Shachar and Lior (Kiki) for their support. Special thanks to Izik Balely and Hal Gordon for all their help.

Part 1: General Jewish Questions and Answers

1. What is tefillin?

Tefillin *(pronounced:t'-FIL-lin, in Hebrew: תְּפִלִּין)* is a pair of black boxes with black straps attached to them, traditionally worn for prayer by Jewish boys, once they become of Bar Mitzvah age. The boxes contain passages from the Five Books of Moses. Some progressive synagogues now encourage girls to wear them as well. Traditional belief states that we wear the tefillin to remind ourselves of our commitment to G-d and the Mitzvot. One tefillin box is bound to the head to symbolize our mental commitment, and one tefillin box is bound to the arm to symbolize our physical commitment.

2. How many parchment scrolls are there in tefillin?

Five: four parchment scrolls are placed in one black box that is bound to the head, and one parchment scroll is placed in one black box that is bound to the arm.

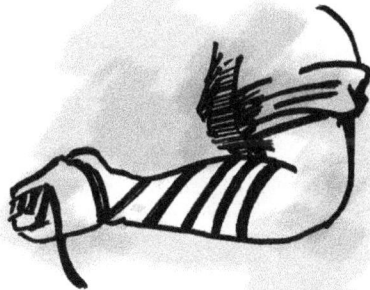

3. What is an aliyah?

An aliyah, *(pronounced:uh-LEE-yuh, in Hebrew: עֲלִיָּה)* literally means "to go up," is when a person is called up to read from the Torah. A Bar/Bat Mitzvah boy/girl will have their first aliyah during their ceremony. On Shabbat morning, usually eight people go up to read from the Torah, and on other days, only three people go up to read. The first one to go up is a Cohen, the second one is a Levi, and the rest are "regular" readers. Sometimes the "regular" readers do not know how to chant the reading, so they just repeat after the rabbi or the chazzan (cantor).

4. On what days might one have an aliyah?

Aliyahs are traditionally held on Mondays, Thursdays, Saturdays (Shabbat), and holidays (Yom Tov). This is because in ancient times, Monday and Thursday were market days, when people would be more likely to come to the synagogue; on Saturdays (Shabbat) and holidays because these are special days in the Jewish calendar. It is a great honor to be given an aliyah. It is actually a Mitzvah to read from the Torah on behalf of the congregation.

5. What is a "Minyan"?

"Minyan" *(pronounced: MIN-yahn; MIN-yin, in Hebrew: מִנְיָן)* refers to ten Jewish adults, (minimum of 13 years old). Formal prayer services require that any Jewish person should not pray alone. The Torah actually commands us to pray in a group. You might find it interesting that most (but not all) of the prayers use the word "we" instead of "I".

6. Are women counted in a minyan, or only men?

In Orthodox tradition, only men are counted; in Reform and Conservative Judaism, women can take part in a minyan as well.

Did You Know?
Women's Roles

Since it's thousands of years old, traditional Judaism is rather rigid about gender roles. Much of the tradition is changing in modern Reform and Conservative synagogues, where women now generally have equal roles and responsibilities to men and are just as able to become religious leaders. Traditions about dress and behavior are beginning to change as well: many Conservative and Reform women wear the kippah and tallit. But unlike Muslims and even some Christians, in the most orthodox traditions, Jewish women have far fewer restrictions on what they can wear than men do, since some of the Mitzvot on clothing does not apply to them.

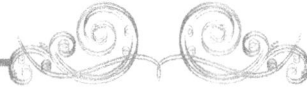

7. How many guests do we need to invite to our Bar/Bat Mitzvah ceremony?

It actually depends on the kind of ceremony you are having. If you are reading from the Torah, you should have at least a minyan. However, if you are having any other kind of service or just a party, it totally depends on you, your budget, and the number of friends and family you would like to invite. Did you know that some congregations give reading and singing parts to the guests so they will feel more involved at the ceremony?

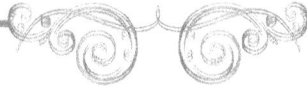

8. What are the Yiddish and the Hebrew names given to the head covering traditionally worn by men?

"Yarmulke" and "kippah" (*pronounced: KEE-Puh, in Hebrew:* כִּפָּה). A kippah is a small skullcap traditionally worn at all times by Orthodox Jewish men, especially when entering a synagogue. A kippah is also worn on special Jewish ceremonies/events such as weddings, funerals, and so forth. If you see a woman wearing a kippah, it means she probably belongs to the Conservative or Reform community. According to the Shulchan Arukh, wearing a kippah is a symbol of "respecting/honoring G-d."

9. What is a tallit?

A tallit *(pronounced: TAH-lit or TAH-lis, in Hebrew: טַלִּית)* is a garment with four clearly visible corners. In ancient times, most people basically wrapped themselves in such garments. Today, because modern clothing does not look that way, we have special garments designed to these specifications, which we wear during prayer. The tallit is worn as a reminder for people to remember to keep the Torah laws. The tallit also symbolizes the feeling of G-d's protection and being under G-d's wings. Over the years, the tallit became known as a symbol of Judaism, and its colors were an inspiration for the Israeli flag.

10. What are the strings hanging from the ends of the tallit called?

The strings are called "tzitzit" *(pronounced: TZIT-zit, in Hebrew: צִיצִית)*

11. What do the strings symbolize?

The Torah tells us: "This shall be tzitzit for you, and when you see it, you will remember all the commandments of G-d to perform them" (Numbers 15, 39)

(במדבר פרק טו, פסוק לט): "וְהָיָה לָכֶם לַצִּיצִת, וּרְאִיתֶם אוֹתוֹ, וּזְכַרְתֶּם אֶת כֹּ־ל מִצְוֹת ה', וַעֲשִׂיתֶם אוֹתָם"

"V'haYA La'chem Le'tzizt, Ur'eetem Otoh, Uz'chartem Et Kol Mitzvot Adonai Va'AHsitem O'tam".

According to tradition, they symbolize that G-d is always with us and watching over us.

Traditionally, there are 16 strings and 10 knots total, which is numerically equivalent to the Hebrew name of G-d.

12. Why do some people have a tallit with blue strings on them?

Traditionally, tzitzit had one blue string, colored by the secretions of a fish identified only as the "chilazon." The modern interpretation of the word is in dispute, so some people believe that they are better off not using any color than using a color that might be incorrect. Others believe that they have found the chilazon, and they make the string with the blue color.

13. What are the small garments some Orthodox Jewish boys wear with tzitzit on them?

Those are called "tallit katan" *(pronounced: TAH-lit kah-TAN, in Hebrew: טַלִּית קָטָן)* literally "small tallit." They wear them every day in order to keep the Mitzvah of wearing tallit. Also, there were times in Jewish history when Jewish people were not allowed to wear tallit, so in order to maintain this Mitzvah of wearing tallit, they wore tallit katan under their clothes.

14. Are tzitzit only worn on special garments?

No. Any garment with four clearly visible corners gets tzitzit. So the next time you dress up in a toga, be sure to tie the right strings onto it!

15. What is a parashah?

A parashah (*pronounced: PAH-RA-shah*) is a section of the Torah (the Five Books of Moses) which is read each week in synagogues on Monday, Thursday, and Saturday (Shabbat). In Hebrew, it is called: Parashat ha-Shavua (פָּרָשַׁת הַשָּׁבוּעַ). The Torah is divided into 54 parashot so that over the course of the lunar year, the Five Books of Moses are read in their entirety. In some weeks, two parashot are read since there are usually not more than 52 Shabbats. The parashot that are read together are the short ones (not more than 157 verses for the two parashot together). Simchat Torah is the holiday that indicates the end of Torah Reading Annual Cycle and heralds the beginning, a new cycle of reading. Some Reform and Conservative synagogues use a triennial cycle, though, so that only a third of each full parashah is read each week, and it takes three years for the entire Torah to be completed.

16. How does someone know which parashah to read for his or her Bar or Bat Mitzvah?

In traditional synagogues, a Bar or Bat Mitzvah boy or girl would read the parashah on the day closest to his or her birthday (at age 12 or 13). However, today many people just do it whenever the synagogue is available, or closest to the end of the Hebrew school year.

17. What is a haftarah?

The haftarah, *pronounced "hahf-TOH-ruh or, Haf-Torah, in Hebrew: (הַפְטָרָה)*, is a part of the later writings of the Bible. It includes books such as the Book of Kings and Samuel, among others. During the time of the Roman occupation, Jews were forbidden to read the Torah, so they chose passages from the haftarah to read instead. Today, we still read it in memory of that tradition. The haftarah usually has a connection to the weekly parashah (Torah portion) that is read in the synagogue.

Did You Know?
Tanakh

The word "Torah" is used to mean a lot of things: it literally means "law," and it can refer to the 613 Mitzvot, or to the Five Books of Moses, or even to the corpus of Jewish religious writings as a whole. A more specific term is "Tanakh (pronounced: tuhn-AHKH)," an acronym for the three parts of the Hebrew Bible: Torah (the Five Books of Moses), Nevi'im (the writings of the prophets), and Ketuvim (historical and other writings, such as Psalms and Kings).

18. If someone only reads the haftarah, can they have a real Bar or Bat Mitzvah?

Yes. In fact, technically, one does not need to do anything except say the blessings. But it is still nice to be able to read from the Torah and haftarah.

19. **Why do a lot of people want to celebrate their Bar or Bat Mitzvah at the Western Wall ("Kotel") in Jerusalem?**

The Western Wall is the last remnant of the ancient Temple in Jerusalem. People from all over the world believe that the "Kotel" is a holy place with a very important Jewish connection to its history and to G-d. That is also the reason that people put notes with their wishes between its stones; they believe that G-d will read their notes and make their wishes come true.

20. Who built the First Temple, and who destroyed it?

According to the Bible, the First Temple was originally built by King Solomon, around 960 BCE. The Temple was built on Mount Moriah in Jerusalem.

It was completely destroyed in 586 BCE by the Babylonians.

21. Who built the Second Temple, and who destroyed it?

Traditional belief claims that the Second Temple was rebuilt by the Jewish exiles who returned to Jerusalem following a decree from Cyrus the Great. Around 20 BCE, Herod the Great renovated the Second Temple.

It was destroyed in 70 CE by the Romans.

22. Where were the First and Second Temples located?

On Mount Moriah in Jerusalem. Mount Moriah is also considered to be the place where the binding of Isaac occurred. Traditional belief says that the mountain is called "Moriah" since in Hebrew the root of the words means "see," and it was there that G-d saw (ר.א.ה) Abraham's devotion.

Did You Know?
A Third Temple

The Second Temple was destroyed by the Romans over 1900 years ago, and there was no Jewish state in Jerusalem to rebuild it until Israel was founded in 1948. So why haven't they rebuilt a Third Temple? There's one major political hurdle: a "mere" 1300 years ago, Muslims built two of their own holy sites, the Dome of the Rock and Al-Aqsa Mosque, right where the Second Temple was, so these would have had to be destroyed to build the Third Temple in the same place. But even without that hurdle, many scholars believe it would be impossible to rebuild the Temple before the appearance of the Messiah, since the measurements and directions in the Torah are not completely clear, and both previous Temples required divine inspiration to build to G-d's specifications.

23. What activities went on in the Temple?

The Temple was the center of ancient Jewish worship, a place for the people of Israel to make pilgrimages, and a place for animal sacrifices.

24. Why don't we sacrifice animals today?

Orthodox Jews claim it is because the Temple has not yet been rebuilt. More progressive Jews believe we've evolved beyond the need for animal sacrifice.

25. What was the Menorah?

The Menorah *(pronounced: me-NOH-ruh, in Hebrew:* מְנוֹרָה*)* was a seven-pronged (also called "armed," or "branched") candelabra used in the Temple. It was made out of gold and was used by Moses, in the desert. The nine-pronged candelabra that we use on Hanukkah (Hanoo-Kiya, in Hebrew: חֲנֻכִּיָּה) is sometimes called a menorah in memory of the ancient Menorah from the holy Temple. The Menorah is the Emblem of Israel surrounded by two olive branches over the word "ISRAEL."

26. What is the capital city of Israel?

The capital is Jerusalem (*pronounced "Yerushaláyim",* *in Hebrew:* יְרוּשָׁלַיִם). It is one of the major cities in Israel. Jerusalem is considered a holy city not just for the Jewish people, but also for Christians and Muslims.

In 2007, the population of Jerusalem was 774,000 (about 12% of all the population in Israel), and the city spread over an area of around 123 km (about 48 square miles).

27. What does "Jerusalem" mean?

It means "City of Peace." Traditional belief says that the word Jerusalem means, "the city that wakes you up to find your inner peace so as to make yourself complete."

Traditional belief also says the word should actually be divided into two parts: "Yeru" and "Shalem." Yeru means the city of G-d, or the city that G-d sees; and Shalem means "complete" in Hebrew.

28. How many names does Jerusalem have?

Jerusalem has more than 70 names. Here are some: "Ir Ha'Elohim" means "City of G-d;" "Ir Ha'Emet" means "City of Truth;" "Kirya Neemana" means "Faithful City;" "Ir Hayofi" means "The Beautiful City;" and "Ir Hazahav" means "City of Gold."

29. What is the "Ark" and where is it located in the synagogue?

The Ark (*pronounced: Aron Kodesh, AH-rohn KOH-desh, in Hebrew: אֲרוֹן קֹדֶשׁ*) is a special closet or cabinet that contains the Torah scrolls. In most cases, the Ark is located on the wall of the synagogue closest to Jerusalem. In America, this means near the east wall; in Asia, the Ark would be near the west wall.

Sometimes, during certain prayers, the Rabbi or a member of the congregation will have the honor of opening or closing the doors of the Ark. While doing that, all people attending the service must be standing.

30. Who decided that Jerusalem would be a holy place?

According to the Bible, King David conquered the city and made it his capital, dedicating a section of the city for the building of the Temple there, something his son Solomon completed. Some also believe that the city was preordained by G-d to be a holy city.

31. At the end of a wedding ceremony, what does it symbolize when the groom breaks a glass by stamping on it?

This custom serves to keep Jerusalem and Israel in our minds even at times of our joy. By breaking the glass, we remember the destruction of Jerusalem and the Holy Temple.

There are many other things you would likely find in a Jewish wedding ceremony. For example: The ketubah – is a contract between the bride and groom, signed by witnesses that indicate the terms of marriage and divorce; the bride and groom stand beneath the chuppah (a canopy- a symbol of a home or a synagogue) and recite seven blessings (sheva brakhot) in the presence of a Rabbi and a minyan.

32. What kind of dancing will you not see at an Orthodox wedding?

You will not see the bride and groom doing a tango together, because the sexes are not allowed to mix freely in public. You will, however, see men and women dancing in separate circles.

33. What does "kosher" mean?

Kosher (*pronounced: KOH-sher, in Hebrew:* כָּשֵׁר) is a list of food products and animals that are allowed to be eaten by observant Jews.

The word "kosher" in Hebrew means "fit," as in food that is "fit" to be eaten by Jewish people. There is a list of these foods in the Torah, in Leviticus 11 and Deuteronomy 14.

Contrary to popular belief, a rabbi does not bless any food in order to make it kosher. Instead, he or she simply watches to make sure the rules of keeping kosher are observed.

34. Which of these options is *not* necessary for meat to be kosher meat (kashroot)?

A) The animal must chew its cud.
B) It cannot be eaten with any condiments.
C) It must be salted.
D) The animal must have cloven (split) hooves.

The answer is B: The animal must chew its cud and have cloven (split) hooves, and it must be salted to drain out the blood. You can still eat it with ketchup, though! Also, it is important to know that for meat to be kosher, there are some other rules that must be followed. For example: fish must have fins and scales (that means eels or shellfish are not on the menu)! Also, most insects are not kosher; any animal that eats other animals is not kosher; meat and dairy products cannot be served at the same meal; and the slaughter (also called shechita) of mammals and fowl must be performed by a trained shochet (kosher butcher), who uses a special technique.

35. How is a Torah made?

A Torah is written on parchment and is completely written by hand. It must be copied, word for word from an existing Torah. In fact, it takes about a year to write one single Torah. There should be no spelling mistakes in the Torah, or it will not be approved for use.

36. Who wrote the original Torah, and what is the oral Torah?

According to tradition, the Torah was given by G-d at Mount Sinai and dictated to Moses to be written years later. The Torah that was given orally to Moses on Mount Sinai were laws and traditions that had been passed down from generation to generation. The written Torah, (i.e., the Five Books of Moses), was written about 40 years after the oral Torah was given.

Others say it was written around the 7th century BCE and is a collection of stories that had been told orally until then.

Did You Know?
Moses and the Torah

Moses is said to have received the Torah from G-d at Sinai, but the Torah is full of events that happened after that, including Moses' own mistakes! Why didn't Moses know what was coming? There are different theories, but in general, it is believed that what Moses received at Sinai wasn't the entire Torah in the written form that we have now, but rather the spiritual essence of Torah, which was only gradually converted into written form as the Jews' historical understanding became more complete.

37. Does the Torah include all the Jewish laws?

Yes and no. There are 613 laws (commandments) (תרי"ג מצוות) mentioned in the Torah, but there are also another seven that were added later by the Rabbis of ancient times, including holidays and stories like Purim and Hanukkah, which had not yet occurred when the Torah was written.

38. What is the Talmud?

The Talmud *(pronounced: TAHL-mood, in Hebrew: תַּלְמוּד)* is a collection of lecture notes, taken down while discussions were going on in the great Jewish seminaries in Jerusalem and Babylon, around the 4th century CE. They discuss interpretations of the oral law of the Torah.

39. Who wrote the Talmud?

A number of authors (in Jerusalem and Babylon) wrote the Talmud over a period of several hundred years. However, the precursor to the Talmud, the Mishnah, is traditionally said to have been written by Rabbi Judah the Prince around 2,000 years ago.

40. In what language is the Talmud written?

Aramaic. (in Hebrew:אֲרָמִית) Aramaic was a Semitic language that influenced the modern Hebrew language as well as the Arabic language. When the Second Temple was still standing in Jerusalem, it was the everyday language of the Israeli region. There are many Aramaic words that have carried over to modern-day Hebrew, such as Aba (dad), Ema (mom), Adraba (even better than that), and Me'Edach (on the other side).

41. Why was the Talmud written in Aramaic?

When the Talmud was written down, Aramaic was the lingua franca (common language) that virtually everyone in the region spoke.

42. What is the Biblical/ classical Hebrew, and why is it different than modern Hebrew?

The classical Hebrew is mostly used for prayer or study in Jewish communities around the world. It was the language in which the Torah was written, and it was used for more than 2000 years. Even today, schools in Israel still teach their students to read the classical Hebrew. It contains the same alphabet letters as in the modern Hebrew, but the words are usually longer and are not used today as the spoken or written language in Israel.

The modern Hebrew was revived by Eliezer Ben-Yehuda at the end of the 19th century in Israel. Ben-Yehuda, who was the editor of the newspaper "Ha'Tzvi," insisted on writing articles

...Continued

and printing them only in the Hebrew language. He was active in raising the awareness of the need for a more formal Hebrew language, and the need to establish schools that teach in Hebrew. Ben-Yehudah was also involved in writing the first modern Hebrew dictionary.

Today, Hebrew is the official language of the State of Israel.

Did You Know?
Hebrew Rules

Hebrew works a lot differently from English. Most obviously, it is read from right to left; also, each Hebrew letter is a consonant, with vowel sounds marked out by special marks accents underneath the letter. Hebrew grammar is just as complex as any other language, but one useful thing to remember is that most words ending in "ah" change to "ot" when becoming plural, such as: "mitzvah" to "mitzvot."

43. What do we mean when we say that something is "Bashert?"

"Bashert" is a Yiddish word that means "destiny," which indicates that something is fated: that it is or was destined to happen.

44. Why do Jewish people give someone a coin for tzedakah before traveling, and should the traveler return the coin?

The coin should not be returned. There is a tradition that "vicarious commands cannot be damaged," meaning that people who have been sent on a mission with orders to give to charity at their destination will be protected from harm by G-d.

45. What is the hand sign some Jews use?

It is called a "Hamsa" (in Hebrew:חָמְסָה), and it is supposed to represent the hand of G-d in Jewish mysticism. The hamsa actually comes from an Arabic word that means the number five (referring to the five fingers). People believe it is an amulet that protects against bad things (like an evil eye) and should be hung on a wall in the house. Some people even put the hamsa in their car with a blessing or a phrase from the Book of Psalms written on it.

46. What does it mean when a word in Hebrew has a numerical value?

Each letter in the Hebrew alphabet has a number associated with it. For example, Aleph is one, Bet is two and so on. Larger numbers are represented by latter letters, such as the Resh, which has a value of 200, or the Shin, with a value of 300. (So "Chai" (in Hebrew: חַי) is 18 because Chet is equal to 8 and Yud is equal to 10). This kind of numerical association is called "gematria" (pronounced: g'-MAH-tree-uh) (גִּימַטְרִיָּה).

Did You Know?
Hebrew Games

Hebrew is full of acronyms, like "Rashi" and "Tanakh", and gematria like 18 for "Chai." These aren't just word games for the fun of it; according to Kabbalistic tradition, there's so much wisdom packed into the Torah that even the order of the letters and their numerical values are full of secret wisdom just waiting to be unpacked.

47. What does "Chai" mean? Why do some people give Bar/Bat Mitzvah boys/girls gifts in multiples of 18, and and why do some people wear it on a chain?

"Chai" means "life". Life is the most important tenet of Judaism: to live. When we raise our glasses, we say "L'chaim," meaning "to life."

"Chai" has a numerical value (in gematria) of 18, so many times you will see gifts of multiplies of Chai (for example: 10 x $18 = $180), or a gold chain with the word Chai in Hebrew:חי

48. What is the Hebrew word for Jews who come from Eastern Europe?

The word is "Ashkenazim" *(pronounced: ahsh-ken-ah-ZEEM, in Hebrew:* אשכנזים*).* The word Ashkenaz is the Hebrew word for: "Germany," so the Jews that came from Germany and Eastern Europe were called Ashkenazic (pronounced: ahsh-ken-AH-zik).

Ashkenazic Jews are the Jewish people who come from France, Germany, and Eastern Europe. The Yiddish language is actually the language that the Ashkenazic Jewish people spoke. Most of the Jews who emigrated from those areas in the last two centuries and most of those who now live in the United States are Ashkenazi.

49. What are the Hebrew words for Jews who came from North Africa, Spain and the Middle Eastern countries?

The word is "Sephardim" *(pronounced: seh-fahr-DEEM, in Hebrew: סְפָרַדִּים).* The word Sephardim comes from the Hebrew word "Sepharad" (ספרד), meaning Spain.

Sephardic Jews are the Jewish people who come from Spain, Portugal, North Africa, and the Middle East. They are divided into two groups: Sephardim (from Spain and Portugal) and Mizrachim (from North Africa and the Middle East). Mizrachim comes from the Hebrew word Mizrach (מזרח) and means east.

50. Are there any differences in the religious rites between "Sepharadim" and "Ashkenazim"?

Yes, one might find differences in the religious rites. For example, many prayers have different tunes while sung in Ashkenazic or Sephardic services.

The two groups also have different holiday customs and different traditional foods. For example, before a Jewish wedding ceremony, Sephardic Jews have a Hena party, which includes songs and prayers. The Mimuna is a traditional holiday of the Moroccan Jews, which is celebrated on the last day of Passover.

51. Why do some people use the word Shabbos and others use the word Shabbath?

Shabbos is only a different pronunciation for Shabbath, used by Ashkenazic Jews. The Ashkenazic Jews use the Yiddish pronunciation for certain words, while the Sephardic Jews were more influenced by the Arabic and Greek pronunciations.

Therefore, many other familiar Jewish words in English were adopted from the Yiddish language; for example, the terms used for the Hanukkah spinning top is called "Driedel" (by the Ashkenazim), while in modern Hebrew, it is called "Sevivon" (from the Hebrew word "sovev"), meaning turning and spinning.

52. Is Judaism a polytheistic, monotheistic, or atheistic religion?

Polytheism is the worship of many gods, monotheism is the worship of one god, and atheism is the belief that there are no gods. Judaism is monotheistic.

53. True or false: There are three major Jewish movements: Orthodox, Conservative, and Reform.

True.

54. Where and how did Reform Judaism begin?

It started in Germany around the middle of the 19th century, after some terrible tragedies befell the Jewish people. Some people felt that Judaism needed to disappear in order for Jews to be safe, but others decided that it should be modernized, or reformed, to create a Judaism that could survive in the modern world.

55. How did Conservative Judaism begin?

Conservative Judaism was created around the turn of the 20th century and was an attempt to create a compromise between strict Orthodox Judaism and more liberal Reform Judaism.

56. What is a Hasid?

A Hasid (or "Hasidic Jew") is an Ultra-Orthodox Jew who follows very strict interpretations of the laws of the Torah and will not compromise them at all for the modern world. In Israel, Hasids (HASIDIM) are commonly referred to as "Haredim," חֲרֵדִים (meaning those who are in awe of G-d). Hasidim is a particular branch of Haredim. The Hasidim follow rules a little differently from other Ultra-Orthodox Jews, and they often incorporate more singing and dancing into their prayers.

57. Who created Hasidic Judaism?

Hasidic Judaism was created in the 18th century by the rabbi named Yisrael ben Eliezer, whose nickname was the "Ba'al Shem Tov," or "master of the good name." He was renowned for his idea that everyone can approach G-d and not just by means of studying of the Torah.

58. Can women become rabbis in Orthodox Judaism?

Yes and no. Generally speaking, Orthodox Jews reject the idea of declaring any woman a rabbi because they believe this would make them more like Conservative or Reform Jews. However, some modern Orthodox Jews have started exploring the idea of giving women the same status as rabbis, but calling them something else, such as "Maharat," which means "leader."

59. What is a mikveh?

It is a ritual bath (pronounced: MIK-veh, in Hebrew: מִקְוֶה), which some Jews dip themselves in for purification purposes. For example, Orthodox married women visit the mikveh once a month. It is also traditional for converts and women who are about to get married to visit the mikveh.

Also, some ultra-orthodox or Hasid boys go to a mikveh when they turn 13.

60. What is a mezuzah?

A mezuzah *(pronounced: me'-ZOO-zuh or plural me'-zoo-ZOT, in Hebrew: מְזוּזָה, or plural מְזוּזוֹת)* is a small piece of parchment, written by hand, which carries a passage of Shema. It is a constant reminder of G-d's presence and G-d's mitzvot.

Traditionally, it is placed on the right side of a doorway. While most people focus on the outer cover (also known as the "House"), the writing on the inside is really what makes the mezuzah (also known as the "Home").

61. Why do we have a mezuzah on our door?

Because in the Torah, the extended text of the Shema prayer says, "You shall inscribe these words on the doorposts of your homes."

"וּכְתַבְתָּם עַל מְזוּזוֹת בֵּיתְךָ וּבִשְׁעָרֶיךָ"
(דְּבָרִים ו, ט)

(Deuteronomy 6, 9) "U' Ktavtahm Ahl Me'zuzut Bey'Techa U'veesh-areacha" This is interpreted to mean that we should hang the parchment from our doorposts.

62. Why do some people tilt the mezuzah?

The Mezuzah is tilted toward the inside to symbolize that G-d enters the room and watches over us as we enter the room.

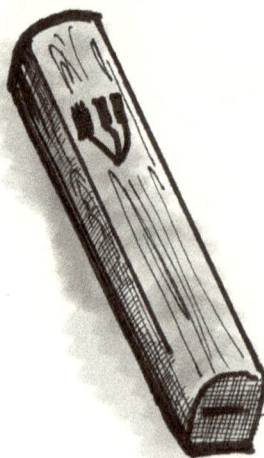

63. : Why do some people kiss the mezuzah?

This is to show their love and respect of G-d.

64. Why don't people have a mezuzah on their cars?

This is because a car is a temporary dwelling, whereas an apartment or home is permanent. However, a mobile home or a houseboat should have a mezuzah if it is your permanent home.

65. What is a yeshiva?

In the United States, a yeshiva is an Orthodox Jewish K-12 school. In Israel, a yeshiva is a place for post-high-school studies, usually run by Orthodox Jews, though the Conservative and Reform movements have their own yeshivas.

66. What is a shul?

"Shul" is the Yiddish term for a synagogue or temple.

67. What is Yiddish?

The word "Yiddish" literally means "Jewish." Yiddish is a language that combines bits of Hebrew, German, and Aramaic into a uniquely Jewish language spoken by Ashkenazic Jews throughout Eastern Europe from around the 10th century until the end of European Jewry, during the Holocaust. During this period, great literary works were written.

Yiddish is written with the Hebrew alphabet. Today, it is mostly spoken by ultra-orthodox Jews and Hasidic communities. Some Jewish movements are active in resuscitating the Yiddish language, such as universities that offer these classes to students.

68. Why are some synagogues called "Temple?"

Because they are considered to be a "little Temple" in memory of the grand Temples that were in Jerusalem.

69. Who was Rashi?

Rashi is an acronym for Rabbi Shimon Yitzchaki, a famous medieval rabbi from France who wrote a commentary on the Torah and the Talmud that has become the standard companion for the study of these texts all over the world.

70. Who was Shabtai Tzvi?

Shabtai Tzvi was a charlatan who lived in Turkey in the mid-17th century. He is infamous for convincing large portions of the Jewish community that he was the long-awaited messiah. Tens of thousands of Jews followed him and expected him to redeem them in Israel. In the end, he converted to Islam under the threat of death and lived out his life in the court of the Ottoman sultan, who controlled the land of Israel at the time.

71. What is Masada?

Masada מְצָדָה is an ancient fortress in the Judean desert overlooking the Dead Sea. After the destruction of the Second Temple in 70 CE some of the Jewish people fled from Jerusalem and went to Masada with their families. In 73 CE, the Romans surrounded Masada and blockaded the fortress for more than two years.

When it became clear that the Jewish people would not survive the Romans' siege, the remaining Jewish people in Masada – approximately 1,000 men, women, and children, led by Eleazar ben Ya'ir – decided to burn the fortress and end their own lives rather than be taken alive and become slaves.

72. What was the Dreyfus affair?

In 1894, a young Jewish officer in the French army, Alfred Dreyfus, was wrongly convicted of spying for Germany, only because he was Jewish. He was exiled to an isolated island called "Devil's Island" as a prisoner for life. The event was a turning point in the relationship between the Jews and anti-Semites in France. Half the French people believed Dreyfus was innocent and was accused only because he was Jew, while the other half believed that Jews were not important or did not deserve equal rights. The famous French (non-Jewish) writer Emile Zola published an unusual open letter to the French president titled "I accuse," which accused the government, military, and legal system of forging documents, lying, and spreading injustice in their investigation of Dreyfus. As a result, Zola fled the country after being sentenced to one year in jail.

73. Who was Theodor Herzl, and what does he have to do with the Dreyfus affair?

Theodor Herzl attended the Dreyfus trial. He was a journalist who never felt too close to his Jewish heritage until the Dreyfus trial. He realized that Dreyfus had been treated badly for no reason other than his Jewishness. In addition, the anti-Jewish statements shocked Herzl, and it soon became clear to him that Jews must have a country of their own. Herzl became the founder of modern political Zionism and is therefore considered to be the father of the modern State of Israel.

74. What was the Partition Plan?

The Partition Plan, passed by the newly created United Nations on November 29, 1947, was a plan to divide the Land of Israel (which used to be called Palestine) into Jewish and Arab countries to avoid war. The Jews agreed, but the Arabs rejected the plan and instead prepared for war.

75. Why is May 14, 1948, (ה' באייר) one of the most significant dates in modern Jewish history?

It is the day that the State of Israel declared her independence (in Hebrew: הַכְרָזַת הָעַצְמָאוּת). This is the date of the official announcement that the new Jewish state, named the State of Israel, had been formally established in what was previously known as "the British Mandate of Palestine."

76. What was the Six-Day War?

This was a war in June 1967 that lasted only six days, when Israel faced Egypt, Jordan, Syria, and Lebanon. Through a surprise attack on the Egyptian air forces, Israel was able to win and actually triple its geographical territory by taking control of places like Sinai, the Golan Heights, Gaza, Judea, and East Jerusalem, all in just six days.

77. What was the Yom Kippur War?

On Yom Kippur, in October 1973, Egyptian and Syrian tanks crossed into Israel and led a surprise attack on Israel, catching them unprepared since so many people were in synagogue or away for the holiday. Israel eventually won the war, but it was devastated by the loss of so many soldiers early in the war.

78. Who famously said, "Send anything that will fly" when discussing Israel?

Richard Nixon, then President of the United States, said this when he was responding to an urgent request from Golda Meir, the Prime Minister of Israel, for supplies to help fight the war. His advisors told him to stay out of it, but he refused, and instead told them, "Send anything that will fly," loaded up with supplies for the beleaguered nation.

79. What is Camp David, and why is it included on a list of questions about Jewish history?

Camp David is a U.S. presidential retreat. While there are many reasons why it may be listed, by far the most famous one is the Camp David Accords, signed by Israeli Prime Minister Menachem Begin and Egyptian President Anwar Sadat in 1978, under the watchful eye of American President Jimmy Carter. It was the first time Israel and an Arab country signed a peace treaty.

80. Who was the first Jewish vice-presidential candidate for a major political party in the United States?

Joe Lieberman, who ran on the Democratic ticket with Al Gore in 2000.

81. Who was the first Jewish member of the House of Representatives?

Lewis Charles Levin. He was elected in 1844 by the American Party and represented a district in Pennsylvania.

82. Who was the first Jewish senator?

David Levy Yulee, a Democrat from Florida. He was elected in 1845.

83. Can a year have 13 months?

Yes, but only in the Jewish calendar. The Jewish calendar is based on a lunar cycle of 28 days, but with a few adjustments to make the lunar year combine with the solar year. The lunar year is determined by the movement of the moon around the earth, and the solar year is based on the movement of the earth around the sun. Because there is a mismatch between the sun's year and the moon's year, and because Jewish tradition is based on the months of the year as well as the seasons, about once every three years there is a leap year, meaning we add another month, called "Adar Bet." That way, we are able to celebrate the holidays in the season to which they are related. Pesach, for example, is celebrated in the spring.

In ancient times, the beginning of the month was determined when two eyewitnesses saw the new moon and notified the Sanhedrin in Jerusalem. The Sanhedrin (Sanhedrin was a council of 23 judges who served during the Biblical period in the land of Israel) then sent messengers to notify everyone that the month had begun.

Part 2: Jewish Holidays and Symbols

84. What is Shabbat, and is it a Holiday?

Shabbat (also called Shah-BAHT or SHAH-bbos by the Ashkenazic Jews) is the seventh day of the week, Saturday. According to the Bible, G-d created the world in six days and rested on the seventh. Jews, therefore, are supposed to rest on Shabbat instead of working. In Yiddish, it is referred to as "Shabbos," and in English it is called "Sabbath."

Did You Know?
The Holiest Day

Even though we talk of the High Holy Days, the most holy day of all is surprisingly common: according to the Torah and its interpretation, Shabbat is the holiest day of all, and takes precedence over almost everything else. Unlike Christians, who often get married as part of a Sunday church ceremony, Jews can't marry on Shabbat; it is a day reserved for rest and contemplation. If G-d can take a day off after Creation, you can take a break too!

85. Why do some Jews refuse to drive or turn on lights on Shabbat?

Traditionally, there are 39 different types of work that are forbidden on Shabbat. One of them is making a fire, which Orthodox and some Conservative Jews interpret to mean starting an electric engine or turning on a light.

86. At what point in the day does Shabbat begin?

Like all the Jewish holidays and every other day in the Jewish calendar, Shabbat begins at sundown the previous night (Friday) and ends on Saturday at sunset (once you see three stars at the sky), with a special ceremony called Havdalah. Havdalah means "to separate," so this is how Jews separate (symbolically) Shabbat, which is a holiday, from the regular days of the week. The Havdalah ceremony includes prayers and blessing over wine, candle, and spices.

87. Under what circumstances can Shabbat be violated?

In the event that a human life is in danger (פִּקּוּחַ נֶפֶשׁ "pikuach nefesh"), a Jew is not only allowed, but required to violate any Shabbat law that stands in the way of saving that life.

88. According to tradition, how many meals are eaten on Shabbat?

There are three festive meals: on Friday night, Saturday morning, and late Saturday afternoon.

89. The month of Tishrei (mid-September to mid-October) is the busiest month of the year. Why?

In Tishrei, we celebrate four holidays: Rosh Hashanah, Yom Kippur, Sukkot, and Simchat Torah.

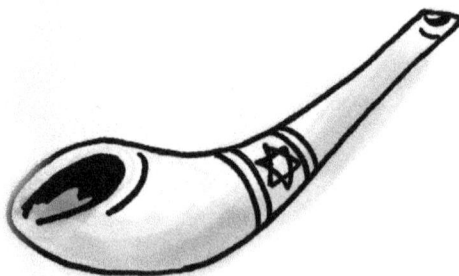

90. What is Rosh Hashanah?

Rosh Hashana is a Jewish holiday, usually celebrated in September. In Hebrew, Rosh Hashanah means "head of the year." It is Jewish New Year. Rosh Hashanah occurs on the first and second days of the Jewish month of Tishrei.

91. What is a shofar?

A shofar *(pronounced: sho-FAHR, in Hebrew: שׁוֹפָר)* is like a trumpet; it is a musical instrument made out of a ram's horn. It does not hurt the ram to collect these, because the horns shed by themselves once a year, and new horns grow back in. The size and color of the horns vary from one ram to another. There are many reasons for blowing the shofar, but traditional belief says that when people hear the loud sound of the shofar, it will remind them of the need to evaluate their ways and correct them as needed. Legend also tells us that the loud sound of the shofar opens the sky so G-d can hear our prayers as we ask for forgiveness on Rosh Hashana and Yom Kippur.

92. What do we customarily eat at Rosh Hashanah to symbolize a sweet new year?

We dip apples in honey (TAPUACH B'DVASH (תַּפּוּחַ בִּדְבַשׁ)). We wish one another goodness and that our year will be sweet like honey and healthy like an apple.

93. Why do some Orthodox Jews go to synagogue very early in the morning on the days leading up to Yom Kippur?

The ten days between Rosh Hashanah and Yom Kippur are called "Ten Days of Repentance" (עֲשֶׂרֶת יְמֵי תְּשׁוּבָה Aseret Yemei Teshuva"). More observant people go to synagogue to say a special prayer called "Selichot," which begs for G-d's forgiveness of their sins before G-d judges them.

94. Why do some Jews think of Yom Kippur as a happy day?

Yom Kippur is a day of atonement (usually in September), when many Jews voluntarily fast all day to try to gain G-d's favor. Some people believe it is a happy day because it is the day when G-d forgives their sins and allows them to start over with a clear conscience.

95. According to Talmudic law, Yom Kippur is the holiest day of the year. Is it a more important day than Shabbat?

No, Shabbat is still said to be the holiest.

96. What are the rules for the temporary buildings (Sukkot) that some Jews build after Yom Kippur is over?

The Sukkah (pronounced: SUK-uh or plural Soo-KOHT) is a temporary dwelling hut that we build at the end of Yom Kippur. The Sukkot holiday is usually celebrated at the end of September or the beginning of October. The Sukkah must have at least three walls covered, and an open roof (made out of branches or bamboo) so one can see the sky. The Sukkah should be big enough for people to sleep and eat in comfort. People should stay in the Sukkah for seven days. The reason for building a Sukkah is to commemorate the time the Jewish people spent in the desert during the Exodus from Egypt. The Torah says,

"בַּסֻּכֹּת תֵּשְׁבוּ שִׁבְעַת יָמִים" (ויקרא כג)

"Ba'Sukkot Te'shvu Shivaht Yamim" Meaning: "You should sit in the Sukkah for seven days" (Leviticus 23).

97. What are the "Four Species in Sukkot," and what do you do with them?

In Talmudic tradition, the Four Species (אַרְבַּעַת הַמִּינִים "Arba'at Ha-Minim") are:

- Lulav (לוּלָב): a ripe, green, closed frond from a date palm tree;

- Hadass (הֲדַס): boughs with leaves from the myrtle tree;

- Aravah (עֲרָבָה): branches with leaves from the willow tree;

- Etrog (אֶתְרוֹג): the fruit of a citron tree;

The Mitzvah of waving the Four Species derives from the Torah. First, one has to recite the blessing. Then, the Four Species are gently shaken three

Continued...

times toward each of the four directions, and plus up and down, to G-
d's mastery over all of creation. The
waving ceremony can be performed
in synagogue, or in the Sukkah, as
long as it is daytime. Women and
girls may also choose to perform
the Mitzvah of waving the lulav and
etrog, although they are not required
by Halakhah to do so.

98. What is Simchat Torah?

Simchat Torah is a Jewish holiday (usually celebrated at the end of September or the beginning of October). The name means "Rejoice with the Torah." It is celebrated in honor of the completion of the annual cycle of reading the weekly Parashah. On Simchat Torah, we read the last Torah portion, and then the first chapter of "Genesis."

This holiday is celebrated in synagogues by singing, dancing, and drinking wine by adults.

99. Can children celebrate Simchat Torah?

Yes, children are welcome to join the celebration; actually, they are even encouraged to celebrate in the synagogues, and in many ways, such as dancing with small stuffed Torah and by eating candy.

100. What is Hanukkah, and why do some Jews give each other gifts on Hanukkah?

Hanukkah *(pronounced: KHAH-nik-uh or KHAH-noo-kah, in Hebrew:* חֲנֻכָּה*)* is a holiday that usually takes place in December. In some places, it is considered to be a minor holiday because people are allowed to work during Hanukkah. It celebrates the liberation of the ancient Jewish community in Israel when it was under the rule of the Greek Empire. Many modern Jews exchange gifts (similar to the Christmas tradition). The traditional reason for gift-giving is because of a law passed by the Greek Empire forbidding Jews from studying the Torah. Jewish children would learn Torah in secret, and when the Greek authorities sent inspectors out to check on

Continued...

...Continued

them, the children would quickly take out some money and a spinning top (known in Yiddish as a dreidel) and say they were playing a game. Another reason is that we encourage children to give tzedakah on Hanukkah, so the money we give them can in turn be donated to the needy.

101. Why are there nine candles on a Hanukkah menorah?

A Hanukkah menorah is designed to commemorate a miracle that happened when the ancient Temple was rededicated. The Jews who entered the Temple could only find a small amount of oil to light the ancient Menorah, just enough for one day. However, the story goes that the oil lasted for a full eight days, enough time for fresh oil to be produced. The ninth candle is called a Shamash and is intended to be a symbolic light, because we are not supposed to use the light of the Hanukkah menorah for anything other than showing off the miracle of Hanukkah. It is important to remember that we are celebrating Hanukkah because of the miracle that occurred

Continued...

...Continued

and not because of the winning of
the war. Jewish people do not formally celebrate the winning of wars.

102. What are the four letters on the dreidel?

On dreidels outside of Israel, they are noon, gimel, heh, (נ,ג,ה,ש) and shin an acronym for the Hebrew phrase "Nes Gadol Hayah Sham," meaning "A big miracle happened **there.**" The driedel in Israel carries the letters noon, gimel, heh, and peh, (נ,ג,ה,פ) "Nes Gadol Hayah Po," meaning, "A big miracle happened **here.**"

103. Why do we eat potato pancakes at Hanukkah?

They are called "Latkes" (*pronounced: LAHT-kees, in Hebrew: לְבִיבָה LEVIVA)*. We eat latkes and other food fried in oil to commemorate the miracle of Hanukkah, where oil lasted eight days.

104. Who was Judah the Maccabee?

Judah the Maccabee, also known as "Judah the Hammer," was the son of Mattathias the Hasmonean. He was born in a city called Modi'in in Israel, the third of five sons of Mattathias the Hasmonean. Antiochus, the Greek ruler, had conquered the land of Israel and wanted to spread the Hellenistic (Greek) culture, so he forbade the Jews from praying to G-d and practicing Judaism. Judah the Maccabee led the Jewish revolt. They fought for the right to practice Judaism, and not be forced to pray to idols. After winning this war, Judah the Maccabee marched into Jerusalem and purified the Temple. Among the ruins of the Temple, they found oil, which lasted eight days.

105. What is Tu B'Shvat?

Tu B'Shvat (טו בשבט) is a date in the Jewish calendar, the 15th of the month of Shvat. It is usually celebrated in mid-January. It's the Jewish New Year for trees (some call it Jewish Arbor Day). Traditionally, Jews eat dried fruits to symbolize the early blossoming of trees.

106. What is a Tu B'Shvat Seder?

The origin of the Tu B'Shvat Seder is in Jewish mysticism, which arose in Safed, Israel, around the middle of the 16th century. Today, it is celebrated mostly by progressive Jews.

Similar to a Passover Seder, a Tu B'Shvat Seder has four cups of wine, but they generally represent the different elements of the Earth and the four seasons.

107. What is Purim?

The word Purim *(pronounced: Poo-rim, in He-brew פּוּרִים) means "lot" (in Hebrew: פוּר –POOR, or, GO-RAL גוֹרָל).* The miracle of Pu-rim occurred in 355-356 BCE after the destruction of the First Temple and before the construction of the Second Temple. It is considered a minor holiday since people are allowed to work during this holi-day. Purim is usually celebrated in March. Purim celebrates the story of the book of Esther, a Jew-ish queen who was married to King Ahashverosh in ancient Persia. According to the story, Haman, chief advisor to the king, was a wicked man who expected everyone to bow down to him. Esther's uncle Mordechai, refused to bow down to Haman because Jews bow only before G-d. Haman decid-ed to punish Mordechai by having all the Jews ex-ecuted, and casting lots to determine the day of the executions. Esther was able to defeat his evil plan by fasting and crying to the king, which convinced him to change his mind and punish Haman. Instead of being executed, Mordechai was paraded around the city in the king's robes when it was revealed that he had also foiled an assassination attempt on the king.

108. Why do some Jews dress up in costumes on Purim?

The catch phrase for Purim is (וְנַהֲפ֣וֹךְ הוּא), "venehefach hu," meaning "it is all turned around." The tables were turned on Haman the evil one; therefore, everything is turned upside down, and we wear costumes to show that nothing is the way it usually is on Purim.

109. What are the four Mitzvot of Purim?

1) K'reeat Me'Gilah - Listening to the public reading of the Megilla (the book of Esther) twice, usually in a synagogue, once in the evening and again the following morning. (קְרִיאַת מְגִילָה)

2) Mishloach Manot - Sending food baskets to friends and family. (מִשְׁלוֹחַ מָנוֹת)

3) Matanot La-evyonim - Giving charity to the poor (מַתָּנוֹת לָאֶבְיוֹנִים)

4) Seudah - Eating a festive meal (סְעֻדָּה, מִשְׁתֶּה)

110. Why do some Jews give each other baskets of food on Purim?

From the book of Esther, it says that it is a Mitzvah to give gifts of food (called Mishloach Manot or Shalach Manos; pronounced: SHAH-lahkh MAH-nohs) to each other on Purim to ensure that friends can celebrate Purim, too. The basket should have at least two different portions of food or drinks and should be given to at least one person, such as a friend, relative, or teacher. People usually add something sweet to the Purim basket and enjoy accepting the baskets, as well. The official time for a person to begin this Mitzvah is at the Bar/Bat Mitzvah age, but it is easy and fun to begin earlier; children in Jewish prekindergarten find it a sweet and happy day, too.

111. What does Pesach commemorate?

The word Passover *(pronounced: PEH-sahkh or Pesach, in Hebrew: פֶּסַח)* commemorates the story of the Exodus from Egypt and the way G-d passed over the Hebrew peoples' homes so they wouldn't be harmed from the plagues. Pesach is usually celebrated in April.

112. What is the meaning of the word "seder," and to what does it refer?

The word "seder" (סדר pronounced: SAY-de'r) is Hebrew for "order," and it refers to 15 signs (words) in a certain order that help us remember the sequence of events in celebrating Seder Pesach. The Seder sequence is:

קַדֵּשׁ וּרְחַץ, כַּרְפַּס יַחַץ, מַגִּיד רַחְצָה,
מוֹצִיא מַצָּה, מָרוֹר כּוֹרֵךְ, שֻׁלְחָן עוֹרֵךְ,
צָפוּן בָּרֵךְ, הַלֵּל נִרְצָה

Kadeish (Kiddush), Rchatz (wash hands), Karpas (dipping the green vegetable) Yachatz (breaking the matzah), Magid (telling the story of leaving Egypt), Rohtzah (washing hands and saying the blessing), Motzi (saying the prayer for eating Matzah), Matzah (eating the matzah), Maror (bitter herbs), Koreich (making a sandwich with Matzah and maror in the middle), Shulchan Orech (the meal itself), Tzafun (eating the afikoman), Bareich (saying Birkat Hamazon, the blessing at the end of meal), Hallel (singing and praying for G-d), and Nirtzah (end of the Seder).

113. What is "matzo," and why is it eaten on Passover?

Matzo (also called Matzah) is a flat, cracker-like "bread" made out of water and flour only. It is deliberately not allowed to rise. It is eaten on Passover to commemorate the Jews' rush to leave ancient Egypt – they did not have enough time to wait for their bread to rise, so it baked on their backs as they ran in the hot sun. Interestingly, Yemenite Jews make soft matzo because the original matzo was likely to have been soft as well, since it was not deliberately rolled out flat and crispy, like our matzo is today.

114. At the Passover Seder, what is the cup of Elijah?

The cup of Elijah is poured in memory of Elijah the prophet, who, according to tradition, will accompany the Messiah when he arrives at some time in the future. There is also a tradition that Elijah visits each Jewish household on Passover night and drinks a sip of wine from each cup poured for him.

Did You Know?
Haggadah

One of the biggest traditions of Passover is – figuring out the meaning of Passover! A book that explains the Passover seder is called a "haggadah," and there are literally dozens of them available, ranging from a Sammy the Spider's children's haggadah (aimed at young children) to the Vegetarian Haggadah. Like most Jewish traditions and like the Torah itself, there is great value seen in finding a personal meaning in the Passover story.

115. What is the cup of Miriam?

According to ancient tradition, Miriam was the sister of Moses. Some say that she was the one for whom water flowed in the desert. Therefore, many Jews, especially progressive Jews, fill a cup with water in her honor.

116. What is "maror," and why do we eat it on Passover?

Maror is a bitter herb, traditionally horseradish. The word comes from the Hebrew word "mar" (מַר), meaning bitter. It is eaten on Passover to commemorate the bitterness of slavery.

117. What is the significance of "charoset," that mixture of apples, wine, walnuts, and spices?

Charoset *(pronounced: khah-ROHset, in Hebrew: חרוסת)* symbolizes the mortar, or cement, with which the Hebrew slaves were forced to build the pyramids for King Pharaoh.

118. What is the significance of dipping a green vegetable in salted water?

The salted water reminds us of the Hebrew slaves' tears. The green vegetable reminds us of the spring season, when everything has new life and flourishes, and we have the feeling of being "Bnai Horin," or "free people."

119. What does breaking the matzo symbolize?

Breaking the matzo reminds us of the splitting of the Red Sea – the miracle that G-d performed to allow the people of Israel to cross the sea in the middle to escape from slavery. Some people say that the noise of breaking the matzo symbolizes the broken bones of the slaves or the breaking free from slavery.

120. What is the significance of the shank bone at the Seder table?

It signifies the strong arm with which G-d released the Jews from bondage. In the Pesach Haggadah it says,

"עֲבָדִים הָיִינוּ, לְפַרְעֹה בְּמִצְרַיִם; וַיּוֹצִיאֵנוּ ה' אֱלֹהֵינוּ מִשָּׁם, בְּיָד חֲזָקָה וּבִזְרוֹעַ נְטוּיָה"

"Avaadim Hayeenu Le'Paroh Be'Mitzraeem, Va'yotzianu Adonai Eloyhenu Me-shahm, Be'Yad Hazakah U'vezroah Ne'tuta".

This means, "We were slaves to Pharaoh in Egypt. And our G-d brought us out from there with a strong hand and an outstretched arm." The bone also symbolizes the korban Pesach (Pesach sacrifice), a lamb that was offered in the Temple in Jerusalem.

Vegetarians only use a picture of shank bone as the symbol.

121. What does eating a boiled egg on Pesach symbolize?

Traditional belief says that the boiled egg symbolizes life and rebirth into freedom from slavery. However, it may also symbolize how, like an egg, people are "soft on the inside" and "hard on the outside" to be able to survive, the same way the people of Israel worked hard as slaves until they broke free and became free people. The egg also symbolizes the korban chagigah (festival sacrifice) that was offered in the Temple in Jerusalem.

122. Why do some Jews lean on a pillow during Passover Seder?

In ancient times, a king or queen would lean back on a couch and be fed his or her food. Because we are considered to be like kings and queens on Passover, we celebrate by leaning back, as if we are also on a couch.

123. Why do we spill wine while we recite the Ten Plagues?

With the recital of the Ten Plagues, each participant uses a fingertip to remove a drop of red wine from his or her cup that symbolizes the spilled blood of the slaves, and reminds us that although now we are happy and celebrating our freedom, we cannot forget the suffering of the Hebrew people when they were slaves.

124. Why do many people hide the afikomen and have children look for it?

This is to get children more involved with the Passover seder. In some traditions, the children actually hide the afikomen and the adults need to "negotiate" in order to get it back.

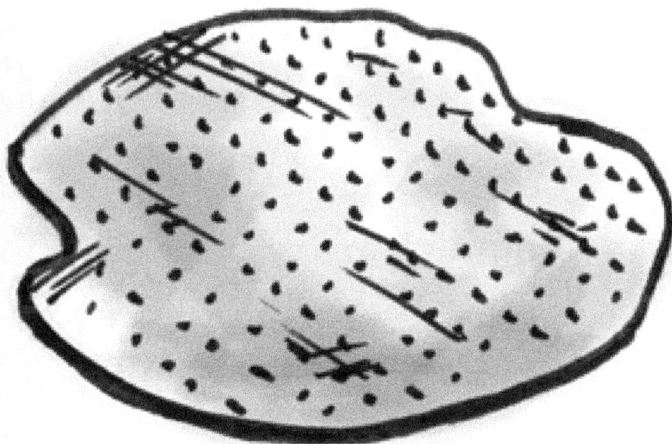

125. What is Yom Ha'shoah?

Yom Hashoah *(pronounced: YOHM hah' shoh-AH, in Hebrew: יוֹם הַזִּכָּרוֹן לַשּׁוֹאָה וְלַגְּבוּרָה.)* is Holocaust Remembrance Day. It is commemorated on the 27th of the month of Nisan in the Jewish calendar (usually in late April or in the beginning of May). This is a memorial day for the victims who died in the Holocaust. All places of entertainment in Israel are closed for the day. Television and radio stations broadcast special programming related to the Holocaust. A special ceremony is held at Yad VaShem, Israel's official memorial museum for the Jewish victims of the Holocaust.

126. What is Yom Ha'zikaron, and how is it commemorated?

It is Israeli Memorial Day *(pronounced: YOHM hah zee-kah-ROHN, in Hebrew: יוֹם הַזִּכָּרוֹן)*. It is commemorated on the fourth day of the month of Iyar in the Jewish calendar (usually in May). It is the day before Yom Ha'atzmaut (Israel's Independence Day), because it is considered a solemn day of introspection to remember the thousands of Jewish soldiers who died so that Israel could be born and remain free and independent.

As on Yom Ha'shoah, all Israeli places of entertainment are closed for the day, and TV and radio stations broadcast special programming related to Yom Ha'zikaron. Ceremonies are held in the cemeteries, and Israeli flags are flown at half-mast. At exactly 11 a.m. on the morning of Yom Ha'zikaron, sirens sound all across the State of Israel, and people stand in silence for one minute in honor of their dead soldiers.

127. What is Yom Ha'atzmaut, and how is it celebrated?

It is Israel's Independence Day *(pronounced: YOHM hah' ahts-mah-OOT, in Hebrew: יוֹם הָעַצְמָאוּת).* It is celebrated on the fifth of Iyar (usually in May). It marks the official date of the establishment of the modern State of Israel and the Declaration of Independence by David Ben Gurion, the first Prime Minister of Israel, on May 14th, 1948.

The celebrations begin with an official ceremony on Mount Herzl in Jerusalem. The ceremony includes a speech by a government official, a parade of soldiers, and the lighting of twelve torches (one for each of the Tribes of Israel) by distinguished citizens who have contributed to the welfare of the community.

On Yom Ha'atzmaut Israelis hang the Israeli flag on their windows, doors, and cars. Often, one sees cars with two flags, the Israeli flag on one side and the American flag on the other, as a token of appreciation to Israel's friendship with America.

128. What is the origin of the Omer?

In ancient times, the Omer was a period lasting from the second day of Passover until the holiday of Shavuot, when people would count down the days until they would harvest their fields. It marks the 49 days from the time when the Jews escaped Egyptian slavery to when they received the Torah at Sinai. Jews recite a special blessing on each day when counting the Omer that states the exact number of that day. For example, on the eighth day of Omer, we would say in Hebrew, "Today is eight days, which is one week and one day of the Omer."

129. Are there special rules or laws to follow during the period of the Omer?

Yes, many observant Jews refrain from swimming or unnecessary bathing during that time. Around the 4th century CE, Rabbi Akiva, a famous rabbi of the time, saw many of his students die in a plague during the time of the Omer. In commemoration of that event, some Orthodox Jews observe some minor version of the mourning ritual, such as not getting married, having parties, getting a haircut, or shaving.

130. What is Lag B'Omer?

Literally, it is a date in the Jewish year calendar (ל"ג) the 33rd day of counting the Omer (usually in May). It is also a commemoration of the death of Rabbi Shimon Bar Yochai, a contemporary of Rabbi Akiva. The day before the night he lay dying of the plague, he had prayed to G-d not to allow the sun to set so that he could teach his students more Torah. The tradition says that the sun miraculously did not set until very late that night, and in commemoration of the event, many Jews light a bonfire to illuminate the night as it was done for Rabbi Bar Yochai.

Tradition says that in honor of the lessons in the Torah that Rabbi Bar Yochai taught, Rabbi Akiva's students stopped dying of the plague after that day. Therefore, Lag B'Omer is a mini-holiday and a break from the rituals of mourning. This is why so many couples choose this day to marry. Also, some observant Jews take their children to Mount Meiron to have their

Continued...

first haircut.

Another reason that we light bonfires is related to the Bar Kokhba revolt, which occurred on Lag B'Omer when Jewish warriors used fire to announce that they had conquered the mountain.

131. What is Yom Yerushaláyim, and why do we celebrate it?

Yom Yerushaláyim *(pronounced: YOHM y'-roo-shah-LAH-yeem, in Hebrew: יְרוּשָׁלַיִם)* is an Israeli national holiday, celebrated on the 28th day of Iyar (usually in May), commemorating the reunification of Jerusalem in 1967. This day also has a religious meaning, during which we thank G-d for being back in Jerusalem, the city of King David.

132. What is Shavuot?

Shavuot *(pronounced: shuh-VOO-oht or shah-VOO-uhs, in Hebrew: שָׁבוּעוֹת)* is a Jewish harvest festival (usually in late May or June), which celebrates the end of the counting of the Omer. It is celebrated exactly 49 days after the 2nd day of Passover. Traditionally, it is also the day when G-d revealed Himself at Mount Sinai and gave Moses the Ten Commandments.

133. What is the Three Weeks?

The Three Weeks (also known as Bein haMetzarim) is the period from the time the walls of ancient Jerusalem were breeched until the First Temple in Jerusalem was destroyed. As during the Omer, many Orthodox Jews commemorate the occasion with some form of mourning ritual, such as refraining from marrying, getting their hair cut, shaving, or listening to music during those three weeks. Some observant Orthodox Jews also refrain from eating meat for nine days.

134. What is Tisha B'Av?

This is the ninth day in the Jewish month of Av (usually in August, pronounced: TISH-uh Be'AHV), when, according to tradition, both of the ancient Temples were set on fire, first by the Babylonians, and hundreds of years later, by the Romans. This is a serious day of mourning for Orthodox Jews. They fast, cry, and pray to G-d. Observant Orthodox Jews refrain from bathing, washing, working, or even learning Torah. Some restaurants and movie theaters are closed in Israel on Tisha B'Av.

Traditional belief claims that bad things happened to the Jewish people in this period of the Three Weeks and especially on Tisha B'av, such as the expulsion of the Jews from Spain in 1492.

135. What is Tu B'Av?

Tu B'Av is the 15th day in the Jewish month of Av (usually in August, pronounced: TOO Be'AHV). It's considered a minor Jewish holiday, as the holiday of love (in Hebrew: חַג הָאַהֲבָה Hag HaAhava), similar to Valentine's Day.

During the Second Temple, Tu B'Av was a happy day when all the unmarried women would dress in white and dance in the fields to find their perfect match or the love of their lives.

Part 3: Torah and Life Cycle

136. What is a Brit Milah?

A Brit Milah *(pronounced: BRIT MEE-lah, in Hebrew:בְּרִית מִילָה)* is a circumcision. It is traditionally done for Jewish boys when they are eight days old. It is a ceremony performed by a certified Mohel, followed by prayers and blessings. It is traditionally a physical sign of the covenant between G-d and Abraham on behalf of the Jewish people to promise G-d that they will keep the Mitzvot and follow the Torah ways.

137. Do girls have a Brit Milah?

Yes and no. Jewish girls are not circumcised, but their birth is celebrated in a special Jewish naming ceremony called "Zeved Habat" (Sephardic) or "Simchat Bat" or "Brit Bat" (Ashkenazi).

Did You Know?
Circumcision

Circumcision is an extremely important Mitzvah. Even non-observant Jews almost always perform this commandment that was given to Abraham as the first Jew. Researchers in the United States have found that circumcised infants are less likely to get sexual disease and less likely to suffer from certain types of cancer. That is the reason that today even many non-Jews are routinely circumcised as newborns.

Uncircumcised men who convert to Judaism can be circumcised in a hospital under full medical supervision; however, a licensed mohel must be present for the circumcision to be religiously valid. Many mohels are trained urologists able to perform this procedure.

138. Why is the Bar Mitzvah held at age 13 and the Bat Mitzvah held at age 12 in our tradition?

Girls physically mature faster than boys and so are considered adults at age 12, whereas boys have to wait until age 13.

139. What does the word Bar/Bat Mitzvah mean?

It literally means "son or daughter of commandments." Someone who is Bar or Bat Mitzvah age is a boy or girl over the ages of 13 or 12, respectively. Bar or Bat Mitzvah ceremony is a celebration of their passage into adulthood, to take responsibility for their own actions.

140. What does being a Bar/Bat Mitzvah boy/girl symbolize?

Traditionally, until the age of 12 or 13, Jewish children were considered to be exempt from punishment if they committed sins against G-d. However, once children reach Bar or Bat Mitzvah age, they are responsible for their own sins. In fact, in some traditional synagogues, a father will say a blessing, thanking G-d for relieving him of the responsibility for the sins of his child.

141. Does someone need to have a celebration to become a Bar or Bat Mitzvah ?

No. You do not even need to have the ceremony. However, the party is fun, and the ceremony reaffirms that you are a part of the Jewish people, so why not have it?

142. Why do some people throw candy at a Bar or Bat Mitzvah celebration?

The tradition comes from Jewish weddings, in which the groom (and in some congregations, the bride) would be called for an aliyah. The candy is thrown to say that they should have a sweet life together. The tradition of throwing candy for a Bar or Bat Mitzvah has much the same meaning – that they should have a sweet life as they grow into a man or woman.

143. What would you expect to find at a Bar/Bat Mitzvah ceremony?

The exact role of the Bar/Bat Mitzvah boy or girl differs from one service to another, from one synagogue to another, from one traditional movement to another, and even from one country to another – for example, services in Israel are different from services in America. However, certain responsibilities are fairly common to all Bar/Bat Mitzvah ceremonies, such as:

- Leading specific prayers or an entire Shabbat service.
- Reading the weekly Torah portion during a Shabbat service. Sometimes the reading is chanted, but it does

Continued...

not have to be. The chanting, of course, is different from one movement to the next and between Ashkenazic and Sephardic traditions.

- Reading the weekly haftarah portion during a Shabbat service. (Again, this can be chanted as well, but it does not have to be.)

- Giving a speech/interpretation about the weekly Torah portion and/or haftarah and emphasizing the commitment to Jewish values (called D'var Torah). Speeches may contain topics such as what it means for the Bar/Bat Mitzvah boy/girl to become a Bnai Mitzvah; a poem or reading that relates to the theme; research on essential questions important to humankind; and, of

Continued...

...Continued

course, recognition of the support of the rabbi, teachers, parents, and relatives.

- Presenting a tzedakah (charity) project that the Bar/Bat Mitzvah boy or girl feels close to.

144. Why do some people try to make their Bar or Bat Mitzvah an occasion to give charity?

After becoming Bar/Bat Mitzvah, one is more responsible for his or her own good deeds. Isn't it a great idea to start off adult life by giving to charity? Tzedakah is a very important Mitzvah. For some people, the most meaningful way to celebrate their rite of passage to adulthood is to undertake a big Mitzvah project and to encourage others to do a Mitzvah, too.

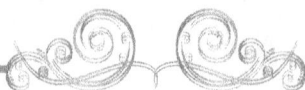

145. What is the Hebrew word for "commandment?"

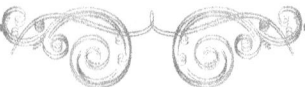

The word is "Mitzvah", מִצְוָה in Hebrew (plural "Mitzvot," Pronounced: MITS-vuh; plural: mits-VOHT

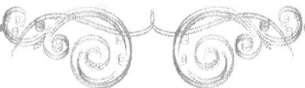

146. How many commandments does the Torah contain?

There are 613 Mitzvot (תרי"ג מִצְווֹת) 365 "negative" (mitzvot Al-ta'aseh or lo ta'aseh- do not do תַעֲשֶׂה מִצְווֹת אַל) one mitzvah for every day in the year) and 248 "positive" (mitzvot Aseh - to do מִצְווֹת עֲשֶׂה one for every bone and important organ in the body, according to tradition). However, since the destruction of the Second Temple, many of these do not apply anymore. There are about 271 Mitzvot that a modern Jew might have to consider, and many of them only apply to certain people or in certain places or times. For example, 26 Mitzvot are only applicable in Israel.

147. What type of commandments are women not obliged to fulfill?

According to the Mishnah, women must perform all the commandments not structured by time, and are exempted from those Mitzvot that are restricted by time, such as praying three times a day and wearing tefillin. This is because of women's traditional domestic roles of bearing children, raising the family, and fulfilling household responsibilities.

148. Under what circumstances can the commandment, "Thou shalt not kill" (לא תרצח) be violated?

Self-defense. The Talmud tells us also:
"הַבָּא לְהוֹרְגֶךָ הַשְׁכֵּם לְהוֹרְגוֹ" (עַל פִּי הַתַּלְמוּד
בְּמַסֶּכֶת סַנְהֶדְרִין עב א, וּמַסֶּכֶת יוֹמָא פה ב)"

"Ha'Bah Le'Horgecha Ha'Shkem Le'Horgo"

This means, "If someone comes to kill you, get up early in the morning to kill him first!" (Berakhot 58a; Yoma 85b; Sanhedrin 72a).

It is important to mention that the accurate translation for the commandment: "לא תרצח" should be "Do not murder." The word "kill" has a different legal meaning than the word "murder." For example, lawful executions and lawfully conducted warfare are not considered murder.

149. What is a Mitzvah Gedola?

Mitzvah Gedola (or literally a "big Mitzvah") means to "Always be happy."

"Mitzvah מִצְוָה גְּדוֹלָה לִהְיוֹת בְּשִׂמְחָה תָּמִיד") Gedolah Le'hiyot Besimcha Tamid.)"

150. Why is honoring a person after they are dead considered to be the "truest act of kindness" (חֶסֶד שֶׁל אֱמֶת "Chesed Shel Emet")?

Honoring the dead is considered the "truest" act of kindness because the dead can never repay the kindness.

151. What did the Israelites say when Moses brought them the Ten Commandments?

"And he took the book of the covenant, and read in the hearing of the people; and they said: 'All that Adonai has spoken will we do, and obey.'"(Exodus, 24:7)

וַיִּקַּח סֵפֶר הַבְּרִית וַיִּקְרָא בְּאָזְנֵי הָעָם וַיֹּ֫אמְרוּ כֹּל אֲשֶׁר דִּבֶּר ה' נַעֲשֶׂה וְנִשְׁמָע" (שְׁמוֹת כ"ד ז')

"VaYikach Sefer Ha'brit Va'Yikrah Be'Oznaey Ha'Uhm Va'Yomeru Kol Asher Deeber Adonai na'aseh v'nishma:" The literal translation from Hebrew for this verse means that the people of Israel replied, "We will obey the laws of G-d first and then hear them."

This means the Jewish people completely trusted the laws of the Torah and promised first to observe the laws of the Torah, and only afterward to study these laws.

152. What is the first commandment in the Torah?

ספר בראשית (פרק א כח): " וַיְבָרֶךְ אֹתָם, אֱלֹהִים, וַיֹּאמֶר לָהֶם אֱלֹהִים פְּרוּ וּרְבוּ וּמִלְאוּ אֶת-הָאָרֶץ, וְכִבְשֻׁהָ; וּרְדוּ בִּדְגַת הַיָּם, וּבְעוֹף הַשָּׁמַיִם, וּבְכָל-חַיָּה, הָרֹמֶשֶׂת עַל-הָאָרֶץ"

Va'yevarech Otam Adonai Va'Yomer Lahem Adonai Pru Ur'vu Umeeleoo et Ha'Aretz UkivShuha Urdu BeeDgat Hayam U'vof Ha-shamayim Uve'chol Chaya Ha-Romeset Al Ha-Aretz".

"And God blessed them; and God said unto them: 'Be fruitful, and multiply, and replenish the earth, and subdue it; and have dominion over the fish of the sea, and over the fowl of the air, and over every living thing that creepeth upon the earth.'Genesis 1:28.

153. Which commandment talks about honoring your parents?

The fifth commandment of the Ten Commandments tells you to honor your father and your mother.

שמות כ' י"א: "כַּבֵּד אֶת- אָבִיךָ, וְאֶת-אִמֶּךָ--לְמַעַן, יַאֲרִכוּן יָמֶיךָ, עַל הָאֲדָמָה, אֲשֶׁר אדוני אֱלֹהֶיךָ נֹתֵן לָךְ"

Kabed et Avicha Ve'et Emecha Lema'an Ya'arichun Yamecha al Ha'adama, Aser Adonai, Elohecha noten Lach.

"Honor your father and your mother, that your days may be long upon the land which G-d has given you" (Exodus, 20: 11)

Did You Know?
"The Lord"

There are many different names and titles for G-d in the Torah. One of the most common is "YHWH," which is pronounced "Yahweh" but is generally not spoken aloud. Instead, Jews often say "Adonai," which is translated in the King James Bible as "the LORD" in capital letters. Since Jews try to avoid mis-using the name of G-d, they must be very careful about writing it down; some won't even write the word "G-d" but instead spell it "G-d." Another tradition is to use "HaSh-em," or "the Name," in place of "Adonai."

154. According to the Torah, how many days did it take G-d to create the world?

It took six days. (Not seven! G-d rested on the seventh day!)

בְּרֵאשִׁית (פֶּרֶק ב, א'-ג'): "וַיְכֻלּוּ הַשָּׁמַיִם וְהָאָרֶץ, וְכָל-צְבָאָם. וַיְכַל אֱלֹהִים בַּיּוֹם הַשְּׁבִיעִי, מְלַאכְתּוֹ אֲשֶׁר עָשָׂה; וַיִּשְׁבֹּת בַּיּוֹם הַשְּׁבִיעִי, מִכָּל-מְלַאכְתּוֹ אֲשֶׁר עָשָׂה. וַיְבָרֶךְ אֱלֹהִים אֶת-יוֹם הַשְּׁבִיעִי, וַיְקַדֵּשׁ אֹתוֹ: כִּי בוֹ שָׁבַת מִכָּל-מְלַאכְתּוֹ, אֲשֶׁר-בָּרָא אֱלֹהִים לַעֲשׂוֹת".

Vayachulu Ha-Shamayim Ve'Haaretz Ve'chol Tzva'am. Vayechal Adonai Bayom Ha'Shviyee Melachto Asher Asah, Va'yishbot Bayom Hashviyee Mee'kol Melachto Asher Asah. Va'Yevarech Adonai Et Yom Ha'Shviyee Va'yekadesh Oto: Ki vo Shavat Mee'kol Melachto Asher Barah Adonai La'asot.

"And the heaven and the earth were finished, and all the host of them. And on the seventh day G-d finished His work which He had made; and He rested on the seventh day from all His work which

Continued...

...Continued

He had made. And G-d blessed the seventh day, and hallowed it; because that in it He rested from all His work which G-d in creating had made" (Genesis 2: 1-3).

155. How many books are there in the Torah?

There are Five Books of Moses (Hamisha Humshei Torah חֲמִשָּׁה חוּמְשֵׁי תּוֹרָה).

The Hebrew names of the five books of the Torah are taken from the initial words of the first verse of each book. Each book is also divided into parashot. Every week, one parashah is read in the synagogue (called the weekly parashah) There are 54 parashot total; parashot are read according to the number of weeks in the year. Here are the names of the five books:

Bereshit: Genesis (בְּרֵאשִׁית), meaning "In the beginning"
Shemot: Exodus (שְׁמוֹת), meanings "The Names"
Vayikra: Leviticus (וַיִּקְרָא), meaning "And He will call"
B'midbar: Numbers (בַּמִּדְבָּר) , meaning "In the wilderness"
Devarim: Deuteronomy (דְּבָרִים), meaning "The words," or "The Things".

156. What do we refer to when we say "Akedah?"

The meaning of the word "akedah" עֲקֵידָה is "binding." The Akedah refers to an event that tested Abraham's faith in G-d. G-d commanded Abraham to sacrifice Isaac, his only son, as a burnt offering. Abraham did not resist and followed the order, binding Isaac to the sacrificial altar. At the last moment G-d sent an angel to stop Abraham from sacrificing his own son and had him sacrifice a ram instead. (Genesis 22:1-24). The Akedah took place on Mount Moriah.

The purpose of the story is to show that Abraham trusted G-d even at the cost of risking his own son's life. Another interpretation to the story relies on Isaac side and claims that G-d protects the innocent.

157. What is tzedakah?

Tzedakah is the Hebrew word for charity. Tzedakah is a commandment that means giving something of yourself to help those in need or contributing to a humanitarian organization.

158. Does tzedakah mean you can donate only money?

No. Tzedakah means you can donate many things, including clothes, food, blood, your time (for instance, by volunteering), and more.

159. **What was the mountain upon which Moses received the Ten Commandments?**

Mount Sinai, also known as Mount Moshe, is located in the Sinai. Tradition states that the exact location is intentionally left unknown so that this place could not be made holy.

Part 4: Special Prayers and Blessings

160. What is the Shema?

The Shema (pronounced : sh'-MAH) is an important prayer that begins: "Shema yisrael, adonai eloheinu, adonai echad" ("שְׁמַע יִשְׂרָאֵל אֲדֹנָי אֱלוֹהֵינוּ אֲדֹנָי אֶחָד"). It is traditionally the first thing a Jewish father teaches his child. It is considered to be the quintessential statement of Jewish faith.

161. What does the Shema prayer say?

In English, it says, "Hear, O Israel: the Lord is our G-d; the Lord is One."

The Shema should be said twice a day – once in the morning, upon awakening, and before bed, in the evening. It should also be said on Yom Kippur and upon death. Originally, the prayer was said by Moses in his speech to the Jewish people before his death.

162. When is the blessing Shehecheyanu recited?

A) At the beginning of a holiday.

B) On the first performance of certain Mitzvot in a year.

C) Upon seeing a friend who has not been seen in at least thirty days.

D) When doing something for the first time (or for the first time that year).

E) All of the above

The answer is E - all of the above. The blessing is:

"בָּרוּךְ אַתָּה ה' אֱלוֹהֵינוּ מֶלֶךְ הָעוֹלָם, שֶׁהֶחֱיָינוּ וְקִיְּמַנוּ וְהִגַּעֲנוּ לַזְמַן הַזֶּה".

"Baruch Ata Adonai, Elohenu Melech Ha'olam, Shehecheyanu Ve'Keemanu Ve'Hagianu Lazman Hazea".

"Blessed are You, our G-d, Ruler of the universe, who has granted us life, sus-

Continued...

...Continued

tained us and enabled us to reach this occasion." The blessing (in the Talmud) is recited to thank G-d for any new or unusual occasion. Jewish people have been reciting this blessing for more than 2000 years.

163. Is a Jew allowed to make a blessing for no reason?

No! A blessing mentions G-d's name, and you cannot use G-d's name without good reason, as it says in the Ten Commandments:

"לֹא תִשָּׂא (ז :שמות ב') אֶת שֵׁם יְהוָה אֱלֹהֶיךָ לַשָּׁוְא.

Lo Tisha et shem Adonai La'shahv.

"You are not to use lightly the name of ADONAI your God, because ADONAI will not leave unpunished someone who uses his name lightly." (Exodus 20:7).

164. What is the correct response upon hearing someone recite a blessing?

This is an easy one: "amen." "Amen" is a word in the Torah that denotes agreement with whatever was said before that. The word comes from the Aramaic language, and its meaning is "true." "Amen" is used after hearing a blessing. However, you should not say "amen" if you have recited the blessing yourself.

165. What is the Hebrew word for prayer?

The word is "tefilah" *(pronounced: t'-FEE-luh)*. When we are praying, we are facing G-d and asking for His help in fulfilling a wish, or expressing our gratitude and respect to Him. Tradition says that in ancient times there weren't any organized prayers, so people made up their own tefilot. Over time, the prayers became more established in texts and in special places such as synagogues.

Dear Jewish teachers and educators,
Thank you for choosing:
"So, what do you know about being Jewish?
165 Jewish Questions and Answers".

We, the professional Jewish educational team in the StoryTime World publishing house, know that teaching Jewish studies can sometimes be challenging. One of the reasons we decided to create this book was to help ourselves and you teach the main terms of Judaism in a more appealing and entertaining way. Below, you will find some ideas that can help you implement the knowledge presented in this book in dynamic and interactive ways. We hope you find this useful and enjoyable.

Suggestion #1: So, what's the question?

Give your students the trivia answers and have them create a corresponding question, like in Jeopardy! For example, let's say the answer is "Jerusalem." Students could come up with questions like: "What is the capital city of Israel? Where was the Temple built? What is the other name for the City of David? What 'is the last word in the "Hatikva" the Israeli anthem?

Suggestion #2: Where's the other half?

Copy the questions and answers on separate flash cards so that you have each question on its own flash card and each matching answer on a different card. Hide the cards in the classroom. Ask the students not only to find the cards "hiding" in the room, but also to match them up together with the corresponding questions/answers.

Suggestion #3: Find your partner

Copy the questions and answers on separate flash cards so that you have each question on its own flash card and each matching answer on a different card. Hand out the cards randomly to the students. Ask the students to find their matching answer or question and sit down with their partner.

Suggestion #4: It's in the story

Divide the class into groups of two or three students. Give each group one question and answer. Ask each group to make up a story and "hide" the question and answer in the story. The rest of the students will need to discover what the question is along with its answer.

Suggestion #5: Touch the answer

Copy only the answers to the questions on separate flash cards. Hang the flash cards in the room on the door, closet, walls, and so forth. Read the questions and ask the students to run to and touch the matching answers.

Suggestion #6: Bingo!

Make Bingo answer sheets for the students. Read the questions and ask the students to X out the matching answers.

Suggestion #7: True or False?

Ask each question as a true or false question. Sometimes, use the correct answer in the question sentences. For example: "Is it true that there are 613 Mitzvot in the Torah?"

Suggestion #8: Two Groups
Boys vs. Girls

Divide the class into 2 two groups: boys and girls. Ask each group to send one student up at a time as a representative. Ask the trivia questions. The representative should know the answer, or the other group gets the points.

Suggestion #9: Something that rhymes with...

While asking the questions, give out hints, such as words that rhyme with the correct answer. For example: "Who enslaved the Jews in Egypt? Here's a hint: it rhymes with "narrow.""

www.ingramcontent.com/pod-product-compliance
Lightning Source LLC
Chambersburg PA
CBHW020244290326
41930CB00038B/330